Dr Terance S

I CAN SeLF PbLiSH

Illustrated by
Milan Ristić

Copyright © 2023 by Team Shipman Publishing Conyers, Georgia

All Rights Reserved

No part of this work may be reproduced or transmitted in any form or by any means, electronic or mechanical, including photocopying and recording, or by any information storage or retrieval system without the prior written permission of Team Shipman Publishing unless such copying is expressly permitted by federal copyright law. Address inquiries to Team Shipman Publishing, 3655 Daniels Bridge Rd, Conyers, GA, 30094

Foreword

People often talk to me about books they have written or want to write. They don't know the next step or want someone else to publish their book for them. I let them know that I can publish their books for them. In fact, the best gift from me is to teach individuals how to publish books themselves. It won't be easy, but it's not that hard. Anyone who wants to do it can, including you.

I want to teach others how to self-publish. There's nothing like taking an idea from paper to print and watching it go through the whole publishing process. Self-publishing is not for everyone. It takes time, resources, energy, and love for what you are doing. I have been self-publishing for over six years now, and I love it. I continue to learn and grow as a publisher. If you decide to take this journey, remember to pace yourself and have patience.

Contents

Foreword 3

Chapter 1: Just Write 7

Chapter 2: Finished Product 11

Chapter 3: The Business Side 15

Chapter 4: Time to Create a Book 21

Chapter 5: Marketing 29

Chapter 6: Launch Day 45

Chapter 7: The First 30 Days Post-Launch
and Beyond 49

Chapter 8: What's Next? 57

CHAPTER 1

Just Write

People come up to me and talk about a book they are writing and haven't finished or an idea for a book they want to write. The first thing I tell them to do is just write. I think aspiring authors really overthink the writing process. Many of them feel that to publish a book, everything has to be perfect, but that's not the case. Before they can begin writing, most writers obsess over paper, pencil, pen, computer, food, drink, clothes, the weather, and the list goes on. But my suggestion is just to start by writing.

Yes, just write! Get those thoughts out of your head. Don't worry about punctuation, capitalization, or sentence structure. Get words on paper. I keep saying paper and pencil because I'm old-fashioned. I like the art of writing words on paper. I love to put my ideas on paper and to be able to see them come alive. Writing gives me a natural pace. There are times when ideas fly quicker than the pencil can move, but there's nothing like the art of putting the pencil to paper.

There is no book without the finished manuscript. You can't publish a half-written book. Take your ideas and write a book! Get through the first stage and just write. Set a goal for when you're going to finish your writing and stick to it. Get the first and most important thing done: finish writing the book.

CHAPTER 2

Finished Product

Now that you have put your thoughts on paper, it's time to shape up your manuscript. If you haven't typed it, go ahead and do so. You probably will make changes, but don't spend a lot of time editing at this point. Instead, focus on getting your manuscript typed and saved as a digital document.

Once you get the original manuscript saved in digital form, begin a soft editing process. When editing, it is important to save every version of the edits separately. Being able to review past edits can improve the overall writing process. If you know a person that you can trust to read and edit your work, ask them to do so. However, make sure you discuss your expectations on editing your work. One of the main things I have learned is to make sure your editor does not change your thoughts. Work with your editor closely to ensure the individual is merely editing, not recreating your work.

The next step is to copyright your material. The United States Copyright Office will register your material. This process can be completed online and costs less than $100. If you don't have the funds for it at that moment, consider a poor man's copyright.

The poor man's copyright can be done in two ways. First, you can place a completed copy of your work in a sealed package and mail it to yourself. This process will register your dated manuscript with the postal service or a notary public. This helps you establish that the manuscript is your property. The second method for a poor man's copyright is to have the completed work notarized stating that the manuscript is your property. Be aware that you can copyright your manuscript separately from your illustrations. If you are not the artist of your illustrations, you should purchase the rights to the illustrations and then copyright the illustrations. You will have to disclose the name of the artist and verify that the rights to the illustrations are yours. Also, make sure to register the finished product (manuscript and illustrations) with the U.S. Copyright office.

Once you have your original manuscript copyrighted, you should begin to look for a professional editor. If you don't have a professional editor, you can easily find one using Upwork or Fiverr. These websites offer freelance services that cover the full spectrum of publishing needs. I have used both services, and the experiences have been great. You can find someone to fit your needs and budget on both.

CHAPTER 3

The Business Side

If you are going to have your own publishing company, you must get a county and state license. I have a great accountant who helped me set everything up. If you want to do it yourself, then go to the Secretary of State's official website. Individuals there will guide you through the process of getting licensed. One of the most important things you need to do is name your company. Once you have decided on a company name, complete a Google search and a search through the U.S. Patent and Trademark Office to ensure the name isn't already claimed. Try to choose a name that is easy to remember. If possible, include your name. You are creating a brand.

The next step is to open a banking account for your brand. Keep your business and personal accounts separate. This separation makes it easier to track all of your business activities. Keep it simple. You don't need a business checking account, just a personal or savings account will do.

I highly recommend you have your own website. I use Wix website services. There are many different web service companies to choose from. Get one that you can set up yourself, and that will keep your costs down. My wife and son initially set up my website. As their schedules got busier, I had to learn how to do things myself. Learning how to manage the website is a good thing because it allows me to make changes at any time. Learn to use the basic operations on your website. There will be times you may want to have a sale, post a picture or just make a change. Knowing how to navigate your company's website without help is imperative. Taking the time to learn to manage your own website is worth it.

Your manuscript must have an International Standard Book Number (ISBN). The ISBN identifies your product when being published internationally. You must establish an ISBN number to print hardcover books, softcover books, eBooks, and audiobooks. Kindle Direct Publishing (KDP), an Amazon company, and a few other printing companies will offer free ISBN numbers, but utilizing the ISBN numbers they offer requires that you give up your rights as the publishing house for your book. It is important to understand that the owner of the ISBN number controls where the book can be sold. Accepting a free ISBN number can stop the sale of your book on your website and any other website, store, or other venues outside of the owner of the ISBN numbers. The content is yours, but your brand will not be known as the publishing company.

I recommend that you buy your own ISBN number. Buying your own ISBN number protects your brand's rights and ability to increase your product's exposure to multiple markets. I buy my ISBN numbers exclusively from Bowker. There are other companies that sell ISBN numbers, but Bowker is the industry standard. In the United States, Bowker is considered highly reputable. There are other companies that offer the sale of ISBN numbers, but those numbers may be used. You won't know that they have been used until you are ready to print your book. By that time, it's too late. You will ultimately end up back at Bowker purchasing a new ISBN number.

Bowker has several packages. If you plan to publish one book (only paperback editions) then buy one ISBN number. If you're going to publish a paperback, hardcover, eBook or audiobook, then buy the ten-pack package. You will save money in the long run.

For print books only, apply for a Library of Congress Control Number (LCCN) from the U.S. Library of Congress before your book is published. The main reason for the LCCN number is to allow your book to become an official part of the U.S. Library of Congress catalog of books. It also helps libraries to locate your book so they can order it. Once you have applied for an LCCN and received it, you can place it on the copyright page of your book.

CHAPTER 4

Time to Create a Book

As a self-publisher, you must select a company to print your book. The two largest companies are Kindle Direct Publishing (KDP) through Amazon and Ingramsparks. There are others, but these two will distribute your book in most of the major retailers and online. They offer reasonable prices for printing. I have always used these two. I used Ingramsparks to print hardcovers books because they do not have a page minimum for hardcover books. KDP prints hardcover books, but the book must have at least 75 pages, including illustrations. A 24-page minimum requirement is the standard for both companies for softcover books. I require all books with my publishing company to be at least 26 pages. Since I began there have been many changes to both KDP and Ingramsparks, but overall, these two printing companies have provided me with great service and excellent products.

Research the type of book you are going to print. If you want to publish a specialty book such as a cardboard or pop-up book, you need to find a specialty publisher. These specialty books are considered hand-craft products and are generally produced in small volumes.

For general hardcover and softcover books, you should research books of a similar genre as yours. Find and review the best and worst-selling books in the genre. Also, consider which would be the best markets for sell of your book. Think about people in your audience. Where and how would they buy your books?

When you upload your final product for printing with the major printing companies, you will be prompted to identify keywords for your book. These keywords will drive the online presence of your book. So, when you search for books of a similar genre as yours, keep track of the keywords you use, and use them as your book's keywords. Always use your name and your publishing company's name as keywords. People should be able to search for your book by your name.

When I published my first book, I had my family format and upload it. This method was not the best. Formatting and uploading are very precise tasks that require training and experience. My family, although eager, was not well trained, and we ran into many errors and problems. If you can format and upload yourself or know someone who is trained, use them if it saves you money. You will need it later. If you are not trained in formatting and uploading, I recommend that you hire professional formatters from Upwork (or Fiverr). It is important that you have a professional-looking final product; mistakes will cost you.

If your book contains illustrations, remember, looks are everything! One of the best pieces of advice I received at the beginning of my publishing journey was to make sure your illustrations are the best and support the overall point of view of the book. Illustrations must support the manuscript! If you are not an artist but want to use illustrations, hire an illustrator.

When hiring an illustrator, make sure you purchase the illustrations and all rights to the illustrations. You should own your illustrations. Some illustrators will ask for a part of your royalties for each book you sell if you do not own the illustrations. Own your words and the illustrations that tell your story.

Your book cover is important! With or without illustrations, your front and back covers matter because readers judge books by their covers! There are templates you can use to create an exciting book cover, or you can hire someone to design it. Your book cover is the first thing most readers notice about your book. Before publishing, it is worth testing your book cover out on a few people who will give you honest reviews. You want a book cover that encourages your target reader to pick up your book. In a bookstore, online, at book festivals, and in most shopping markets, your book cover will compete with thousands of other options. It is worth the time and money to make sure your book cover stands out and draws in customers.

Once you have successfully uploaded your book, order proof copies of it. This process is exciting. It will be your first look at YOUR BOOK! I usually order three to five copies and have a Beta group read the book before the launch date. A Beta group is a group of people who give honest opinions about your book. They will also catch mistakes that you and your editor missed. My Beta group always tells me the good or bad qualities of my books. I also take time to read and reread my proof copy. I have found many errors in this process. With the feedback from the Beta group, make any adjustments, corrections, and changes that improve the book. Then re-upload the book, and order another set of proofs. With your second set of proofs, utilize the Beta group again, continually checking for errors and areas of improvement. When you feel that your book is ready and error-free, go ahead and set your launch date for the book.

Before selecting a launch date, consider the following:

1. Launch around a payday—usually the 1st or 15th of the month or the 15th. People spend money when they have money! And that tends to be around payday!
2. Stay away from launching around holidays. Extra spending money is usually allocated for holiday activities during that time.
3. Tuesdays and Fridays are good days to launch. Tuesdays are already associated with movie and book releases in the US market. And Fridays are associated with weekly pay periods and nondiscretionary spending.

Again, you are competing with millions of ways that people can spend money. You want to optimize the probability that people see your book when they are ready to spend their money!

CHAPTER 5

Marketing

One of the most important things about self-publishing is marketing. There is no direct science that will guarantee success. You're going to have to spend money. However, you should research to spend your money wisely. Many companies and services will tell you that they will increase your book sales through their promotion strategies, which include blasting your book on their social media pages, reviewing your book, posting author interviews, or including you on their blogs and podcast. I have done many of these over the years. Some of them helped me boost my brand, but others were a waste of money. Some worked to help build my social media presence. Actually, you can do much of this promotion yourself.

Google your name and brand name to see what information shows up. Look at images associated with your name and brand. You can increase your online presence without hiring a marketing specialist. There are some basic strategies that will increase your online footprint.

First, name all your social media pages with the same title (or handle). All my social media sites are named after me: Terance Shipman. Some authors use their book titles or publishing company as their social media handles, and that is not a bad idea. In my case, I knew I would publish more than one book and wanted to make sure that no matter how many books I published, all would be linked back to me. I made this concept simple by housing all my publishing works under my name. Any online search for my name leads to all titles under Team Shipman. This strategy is all part of building a brand.

Secondly, everything I post on social media adds to my Google search profile. You want to be seen as much as possible as an author, so try to keep things about your private life out of the main steam. Share non-book-related things, because everything shouldn't be about your books. Generally, these things should lead back to the major themes that are at the core of your books. For example, my books are for children, so when I post non-book-related content on my social media, it provides information that will engage readers who are more likely to be interested in children's books, and (hopefully) leads them back to my books.

Another marketing strategy is to research at least three authors and see how their social media pages are set up to determine if anything they do can work for you. If you feel that it can, emulate their style.

Finally, always review comments left on your social media. Expect positive and negative comments. Always respond to positive comments. Simply liking a comment shows that you see and appreciate it. Approach the negative comments with grace. If the comments are inappropriate, block the user and delete the comment. If the comment expresses a general dislike of your product, graciously thank the commenter and move on.

Although all my social media pages are named after me, I also maintain a social media page for my publishing company, "Team Shipman Publishing" (TSP), and manage a social page called "The Real PTA" on Facebook. The TSP page was designed to highlight the brand, while the Real PTA was set up to have posts and interactions on educational topics. I also promote my books on these pages. Managing many social media pages increases your book's exposure to more shopping markets. Increased exposure increases sales!

Another marketing strategy I have employed is also based on social media. I join groups on Facebook that are related to authors, promotion, and education. Joining these groups has helped me as an author. I learned how other authors promote their works. I see how they utilize social media to increase their exposure. I also learned about the limitations of social media.

Some social media pages are set up for authors to promote their works, but I question if these pages are ever seen by anyone other than other authors. I also learned to use care when promoting my material on other users' pages and groups. Some pages and groups have rules that can restrict the promotion of your work. When you try to promote your book on these pages, you are considered spam and may be reported to Facebook Monitors. The next thing you know, you're in Facebook Jail—restricted on the entirety of Facebook. Your ban from Facebook can be days or weeks, and during that time you lose your ability to post and advertise your work. So, make sure you review the rules of other users' pages and determine if you can abide by those rules before you join the group and post.

Even after you have entered the social media world to promote your book, you must have a plan of use that will increase your book sales. The following is a list of marketing strategies I have used:

1. Email, Text List, and Facebook Messenger. These are easy ways to send ads and information about your books to family and friends. But be warned: building a reliable email list can be difficult. Many people will unsubscribe and block you once they receive a few messages. Do not overuse these methods. Use it for launches and special sales of your product.

2. Goodreads Giveaway. Goodreads is a website/app that allows readers from around the world to review and rate books. The site also connects readers to authors and allows them to communicate. Readers can ask questions of the authors about specific works. Users

can follow other users who have similar reading preferences to learn about new books. It's a great way to market your book. I have used Goodreads several times to promote books.

One of the best promotions that authors can utilize through Goodreads is the book giveaway. You can do print or digital giveaways. Goodreads offers several package options for authors to choose from for giveaways, and members of Goodreads are notified about the giveaways. These giveaways help spread the word about your book. Most winners leave a review of your book. I have found that readers participate when the prize is a print book, but digital book giveaways garner more reviews.

Digital giveaways are done through Kindle, and Goodreads requires you to give away 100 copies. I run most of my giveaways for 30 days and post them on all my social media outlets.

I use social media to promote my Goodreads giveaways. There are Goodreads giveaway groups on social media. I advise authors to join these groups and post about your giveaways daily. This method easily increases the exposure of your book.

Once a print book giveaway is completed, mail the books to the winners as soon as possible. Include a nice note with the book to thank the reader for participating and ask for a review of your book. Make sure you include the link or a QR code for the review site. Digital giveaway books are all Kindle books and will automatically be delivered to the user's Kindle library as soon as the giveaway is over.

3. Videos. When marketing any publication, videos can easily be used. Videos are popular and reach diverse markets for your publications. You can use videos to promote an individual book, a series of books, a launch, a special sales price, or a promotional event. You can hire a freelance service to make your videos, or you can make them yourself. I make

my own video ads, utilizing easy-to-use apps on my iPhone. There are several apps that can help you create videos, such as iMovie, Ripl, Adobe Premiere Pro, TikTok, and Instagram. Whatever you decide to do, make sure it looks professional. Again, the presentation of your book is important. Ideally, promotional videos should be between 30 to 60 seconds in length and highlight your books. YouTube is a great way to publish your videos and gain more exposure to your books. Your videos will come up in Internet searches under your name or brand. I encourage you to start a YouTube channel and upload the videos that you have made for your book. You can advertise your videos on YouTube also. YouTube is constantly changing. Check for changes quarterly when it comes to advertising.

4. Blog, Podcast, and Interviews. I have my own blogs and podcasts on my website, and both are called "Mr. Shipman's Class." Although both are fun ways to promote your work, the biggest challenge is creating new content.

You have to commit to producing content on a regular basis because you want users to return to your site regularly.

Blogs are great ways to build content on your websites and social media. You can write your own blogs, covering content that is related to your books. You can also have other writers develop content for you. Many writers will happily write a short blog for you free of charge when asked. Podcasts are a great way to reach a much wider audience worldwide. You can produce a very professional-looking podcast utilizing a good cellphone without the need for expensive apps to edit and publish it. Keep the content related to areas that are similar or related to the content of your book. Interviews can be used to promote your books too. Interviews can be done in a variety of ways. You can be interviewed virtually on other performers' blogs, vlogs, and podcasts. You can also do print interviews with writers who publish online newsletters and magazines. Also, you can orchestrate your own interview, develop questions, acquire your own interviewer, and publish the interview on your social media sites and web pages. But always remember the goal of your blogs, podcasts, and interviews is to increase exposure to your books and drive buying customers towards venues where they can purchase your books.

Whether it's a blog, podcast, or interview, always do your research. If you are asked to be a guest on someone's blog, research the production. Find our information about them. How many viewers do they have? Are their viewers the typical buyers of your content? Are they asking you to pay for the blog, podcast, or interview? And if they are, will that initial investment you make get a reasonable return? Also, on all blogs, podcasts, and interviews make sure you have a link or say all venues where a buyer can purchase your book. Make it easy for people to purchase your books!

5. Book Reviews. The success of your book can be enhanced by book reviews. They give po-

tential readers a glimpse into your content and allow them to see what someone thinks about your work. However, you must be able to accept both good and bad reviews. Team Shipman Publishing has received some fantastic, professional reviews from readers who understood the book and added great insight to my work. Other reviewers hated my books. Either way, all reviews are needed, and they are very hard to come by. Not having reviews for your books suggests that you have no one willing to read your content, and that is the exact opposite of what you want. So, you must work to encourage readers to write reviews of your works!

I give away free books and ask readers to leave a review. I always make sure readers have a link to all venues so they can review my book after they have read it. These are simple ways to make it easy for people to review your book.

Placing ad cards with copies of books you mail to buyers is also a way of encouraging readers to give reviews. Make sure you list links to several online sites where reviews can be listed. Creating scannable QR Codes that take the user directly to the site is another way to promote reviews. These codes should be on the ad cards and any signs you use at promotional events. Remind readers that they can leave reviews on any site that sells your book or provides opportunities for sharing it. Again, all reviews are good reviews!

There is one area of reviews that I recommend you use caution. Be careful about buying reviews. As computer algorithms associate you with your book and being an author, you will receive pop-up ads, emails, post-response messages, and social media video feeds offering reviewing services. First, these reviews cost money and may or may not be helpful. Even if the review is actually completed, you should still question it. Where will it be posted? Is that site of posting attracting your targeted market? Do that site bring in enough viewers to justify paying for the review? Often times these paid reviews include being published on sites that are not American-based, and they engage with audiences not interested in American books.

Finally, don't manufacture reviews of your own books. Amazon and many other sites will take down your reviews or any others they suspect were paid. The bottom line is to continue encouraging your readers to leave reviews.

6. Presales. Purchases of your book made before the actual launch date count. Presales create a buzz and excitement about the book. During my pre-launch days, I always use various social media outlets to promote presales. When I do this, I make sure potential buyers have a link to all venues just in case they want to make presale purchases. I make it easy for people to pre-purchase the book! You can encourage presales by lowering the introductory cost of the book. It does not have to be a huge decrease, but enough to boost your sales. I have always done presales with my

books. The results have been mixed. I have found more success with combining presales with Goodreads giveaways. This combination will at least put your book in the hands of potential readers who will get exposure to your book and might leave a review early in your book's life. People get excited to buy a book that is not out yet.

CHAPTER 6

Launch Day

One of the most exciting days is the launching of a new book. All the hard work has come to this one day. I've had launch days where sales were great and other launch days where I had problems with publication.

I like to say launch day rather than release day. I think of the release as launching a rocket into space. It is a positive affirmation of my hopes for my book! You want the sale to be so great that it launches you and your book into that rare space of best seller!

Pre-Launch Days

During the days leading up to your launch, consider doing the following:

1. Ask family, friends, and your Beta group to share the book cover and link to the book on their social media pages. They can do it the day before or the day of the launch.

2. Post links to any book reviews that you may have on your social media.

3. Have a 5 or 10-day countdown until launch day. During the countdown, blast the internet and social media with video advertisements and sneak previews of artwork from the new book. Add interesting facts and tidbits about the characters of the new book or you as the author. Have fun with it and try to engage as many viewers as possible. If you choose to do this, please make sure you respond to all comments, remembering that the driving algorithms promote posts that receive more engagement.

4. Lastly, enjoy your launch day. You published a book, and now people all over the world can read it. Yes, you have a lot of work ahead of you, but celebrate! You self-published a book!

CHAPTER 7

The First 30 Days Post-Launch and Beyond

Facebook and Instagram Advertisements

Your book has been launched, now you have to work to sell it. Remember everyone doesn't want to buy your book. Even the people in your targeted audience may resist purchasing your book. There are thousands of books that appear on a search for books like yours. It is your job to make your book stand out, be at the top of the search, and arouse curiosity about your book in readers. Always sell your book as unique and special. A simple and effective way to build an audience is through social media advertisements. Are ads a guarantee for selling books? No, the only guarantee is there are no guarantees in this business. Ads have helped get my books noticed and seen by people around the world. I don't recommend spending a lot of money, but ads continuously run to get results.

How to Set Up Ads on Facebook

1. Acquire a Facebook Ads manager account.
2. Create an ad-on manager (picture or video).
3. Select an objective by determining the purpose of the ad. (Example: to list sites for purchase; to introduce the content of the book).

4. Choose your target audience. This includes location (city/county/region), demographic of the audience (parent/single young adult, elderly), and interest (reader/educators/audiobook enthusiasts).
5. Set a budget and time duration for the ad.
6. Create your ad.
7. Allow your ad to run for at least a week before making changes. During that week monitor your ad to check performance. Each social media site has an insight function that will allow you to track whom the ad is reaching, what their engagement level is with the ad, and when the ad is being viewed. Use this information to adjust your ads.

How to Set Up Ads on Instagram

1. Select the ad you want to boost (picture or video).
2. Choose your target audience.
3. Set your budget and time duration.
4. Keep track of insights, and make adjustments to highlight things that work overtime.

5. When you run ads (boost) make sure you have a link to all venues where a buyer can purchase your book. Make it easy for people to purchase the book! You want your customers to be able to go directly to your book. Because viewers usually need to see an ad multiple times before they buy the product, try to run your ads for a 7–10-day period directed at your target market.

Events

Events are very important for your business. An event is a physical marketplace where you go to sell your books. These can be book shows, bookstores, conventions, or conferences. I have done it at several events. At the beginning of my self-publishing journey, I generally took a financial loss at these events. Now I select events differently based on my experiences, and I am seeing more and more profit from events. Here are some things that I have learned about events.

1. Beware of high-cost events that are only for one day and a few hours. Calculate the hour-

ly rate that you must earn to cover the cost of the event. Then consider how many books you need to sell to cover the cost of the event and make a profit. Include the value of your time when doing these calculations. Your time is your money!

2. The location of the event must have a lot of foot traffic (malls, festivals, fairs, and conferences). Events held in schools on weekends have very little traffic. You can't make a sale when you don't have buyers. Ask the event planner for evidence of buyers, such as pictures and videos of previous years. Annual events are usually good ones. They tend to have a return crowd that comes prepared to spend money!

3. Many outdoor events don't refund your money when it rains, and you do not want your books exposed to the rain or heavy wind. Tents do very little to protect your books from blowing rain.

Bookstores

All authors dream of having their books in bookstores. In fact, one of the most definitive moments for all authors is walking into a bookstore and seeing their books on the shelf! It is what many authors aspire to, but it does not necessarily mean the author is successfully earning money from the sales of the book. The publisher controls the price and profit of the book, and often large publishing companies control bookstores, particularly big box bookstores. Smaller, privately owned bookstores are not dominated by publishing companies as mainstream big box stores, but they still have limitations and problems that self-publishers must be aware of if they want to earn as much as possible for their books.

As a self-publishing company and author, retail placement can be done, but it usually comes at a high cost. Some independent bookstores will ask you to preview your book for free. The preview usually takes a while. During that time, your book is not on the shelves of their stores, and you do not have the money from the sale of those books. Also, during independent bookstore preview time, you must get your book to them. If you mail it to them, include a self-addressed stamped envelope. Without a return envelope, you will not get your book back if the stores choose not to place it on their shelves.

Most independent bookstores will contact you and let you know if your book is acceptable. You will be offered a contract stating that you agree to a 60/40 royalties split. You will get 60% of the sales, and the bookstore will get 40%. Most independent bookstores will ask you for five books. The books will sell for the price the bookstore owner chooses, and the profits may vary. Bookstores are supposed to contact you once all the books have sold, but they have no incentive to do it quickly unless there is a high demand for your book. To ensure you receive the profits from your books, you must check with the bookstore often to see if any of your books have sold. I recommend you monitor the sales quarterly. If possible, I recommend a physical check because again, the bookstore is not motivated to give you your profit unless your books are in high demand. Make sure you make your money. Don't just let someone else make money off your hard work.

Audiobooks

One of the growing markets for authors is audiobooks. It is a great way to give readers multiple angles of exposure to your books. The audiobook market is a huge growing market and source of revenue. I use Audiobook Creation Exchange (ACX) which is owned by Amazon to distribute my audiobooks. Your book has to be published first before you can begin uploading to ACX. I have my son produce my audiobooks. ACX does have talent and producers for hire, but this can be expensive and difficult to control. I recommend producing your audiobook yourself. If you have access to a quality recording sound system (found on most laptops), a sound studio, (a soundproofed room), a quality microphone (which can be purchased at any electronic store), and someone to narrate the book, you can produce your own audiobook with a little work. ACX has strict requirements for uploading, so make sure you have someone who really knows about recording audio. Once you are approved, ACX will give you free audiobooks to give to reviewers. You can send a code to be redeemed by reviewers. This is to help you get reviews and build an audience.

CHAPTER 8

What's Next?

You have now self-published a book, so the big question is what's next? Do you plan on writing more books? Are you going to do a book tour, or was this experience too much for you? The self-publishing business is not easy. Most writers give up after one or two books. Many of the authors that came out with books when I first started are no longer publishing. A few self-publishing authors have been signed by major publishing companies.

I continue to move forward each day and learn more about the self-publishing business. I still go days without selling a book, but I also have days that I sell almost all the books I keep in my business stock. You have to find your niche and work it.

Spend your money carefully and wisely. No one else can work your dream like you can. Keep writing and believing in your dream. It doesn't have to cost a lot of money, but you will have to put in the time. Always study the latest trends in the business. Lastly, have fun and enjoy the experience. There is nothing like having people tell you they love your book. That feeling feels great every time.

Maintenance of Your Self-Publishing Company

So, you've decided to continue publishing books, Well that's great! Here are some simple maintenance tips that will help you grow your brand and see increased profits:

1. Decide if you want only to publish your works or if you want to bring in new authors.

    By this point, you know how to publish and market your works. You have established a target market and built relationships with illustrators, formatters, editors, and other business-related personnel. They work for the betterment of your books and brand. To take a new author, you have to be willing to establish all of those for another person, and you generally do not want to share your personnel with your new authors. To do so, may overwork your personnel and place your new author in direct competition with your works.

Taking on a new author is a huge undertaking, so consider all the pros and cons before you begin. You should have very honest conversations with the potential new author about marketing and promotion. If you've published your own works, you know that creating the book is easier than promoting the book. If you take on a new author to publish, you have to determine if you are willing to promote the book as well. And, you have to determine a fair market price for the services you are willing to provide.

2. Determine how you will stock your company. Stocking through online platforms is an option. However, if you sell your book on most online platforms such as Amazon, you must be cognizant of the cost of the book. These online platforms take their profit before they give you yours. So, unless you are selling thousands of books on their platforms, you will only see a small profit.

My recommendation is to stock your books at home and take accountability for the distribution of your book. You can purchase your books from your printer at a much lower cost than the general public can. Stock your books at home and drive as much business as possible to your website for sales. Utilize a website that provides secure encrypted payment options. Check it daily and send customers their books expeditiously.

3. Monitor your printing companies' site regularly.

Milton Keynes UK
Ingram Content Group UK Ltd.
UKHW021037100823
426647UK00016B/329